My First
Dot-to-Dot

Illustrated by Sonia Baretti & Maria Neradova

Written by Elizabeth Golding

Designed by Anton Poitier & Ben Potter

B.E.S.
PUBLISHING

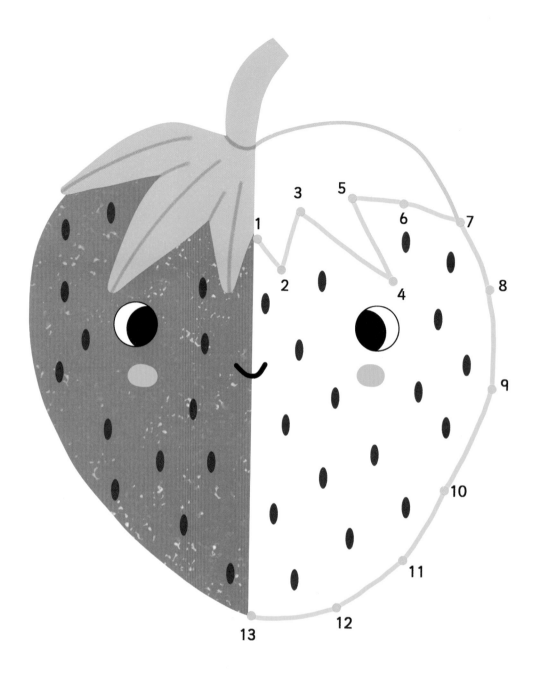

All inquiries should be addressed to:
B.E.S. Publishing
250 Wireless Boulevard
Hauppauge, New York 11788
www.bes-publishing.com

ISBN: 978-1-4380-1002-1

Date of Manufacture: June 2019
Place of Manufacture: Shenzhen Caimei
    Printing Co., Ltd

Printed in Shenzhen, China

15 14 13 12 11 10

Go dotty!

This book is jam-packed with lots of fun dot-to-dot puzzles. Use a pencil, felt-tip pen, or colored pencil to follow the numbers in each dot-to-dot. There is a question to answer on each page too!

The puzzles get harder as you turn each page. The last puzzle has 100 dots! Don't worry if you get stuck with anything, the answers are at the back of the book.

The dot-to-dot pictures look good colored in, too. Choose your favorite colored pencils or felt-tip pens and color in as little or as much as you like.

How many wheels do you see?

I see ⬜ w_____.

Where do you see me?

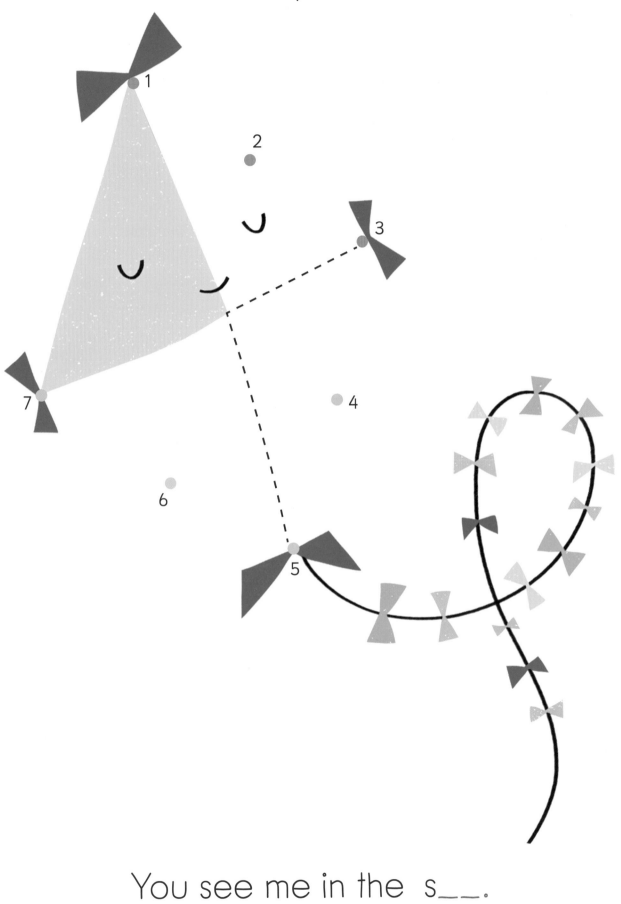

You see me in the s__.

What color is the cherry on top?

The cherry is r_d.

Would you eat me?

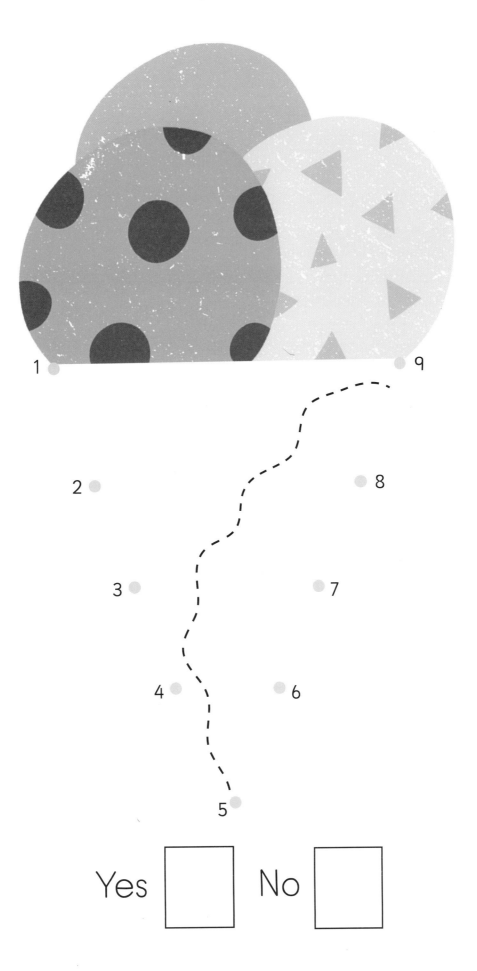

Yes ☐ No ☐

What did the mouse eat?

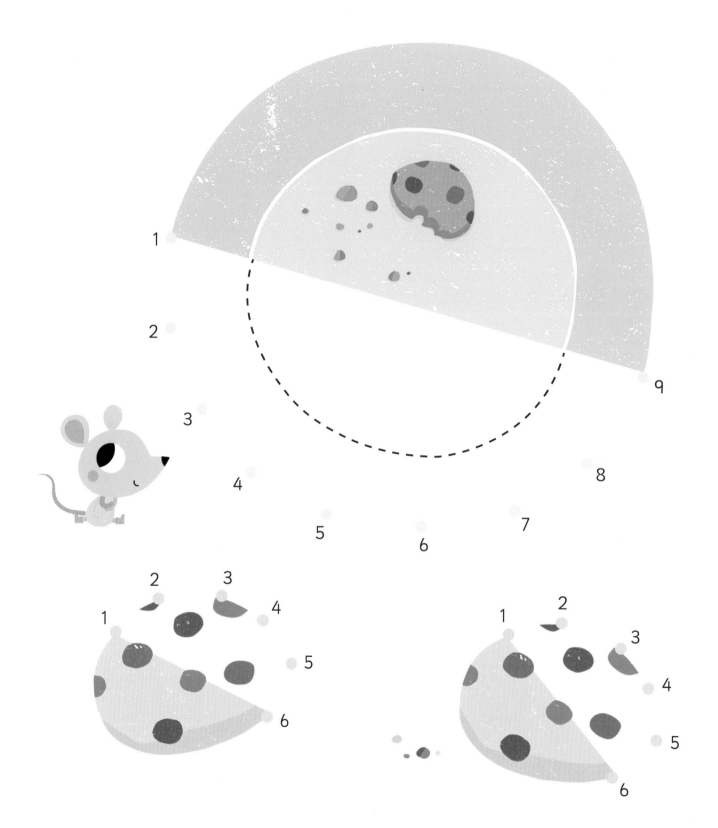

The mouse ate my c_____s.

What am I?

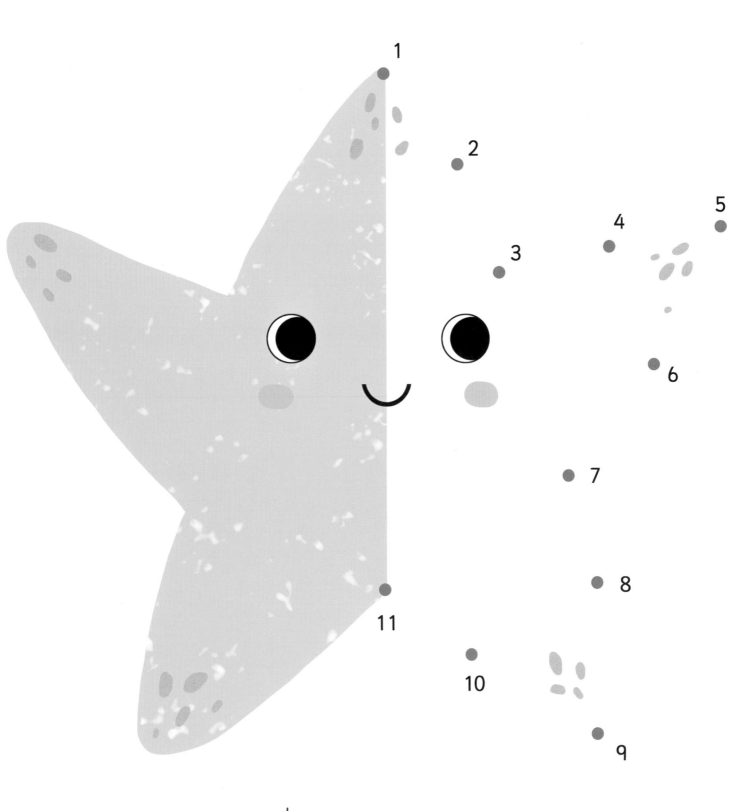

I am a s__r.

How many bubbles do you see?

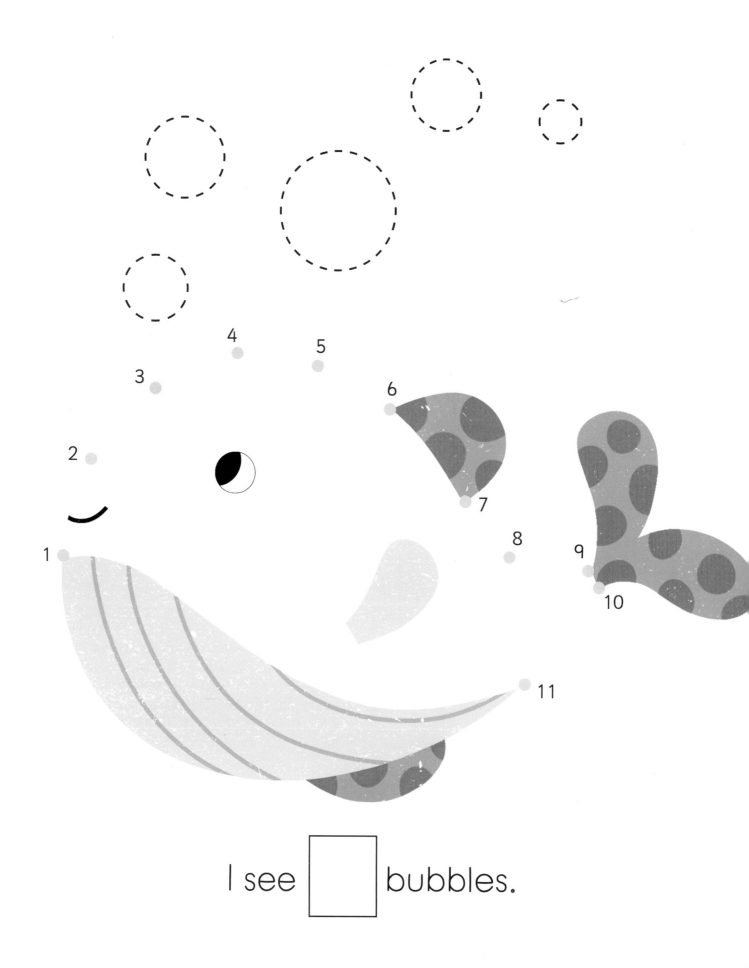

I see ☐ bubbles.

What am I called?

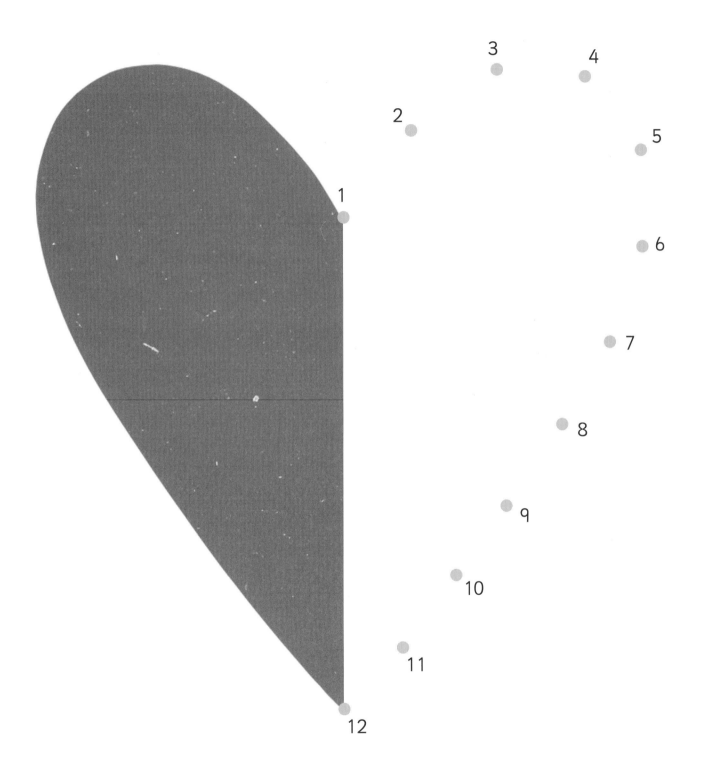

I am called a h___t.

What colors am I?

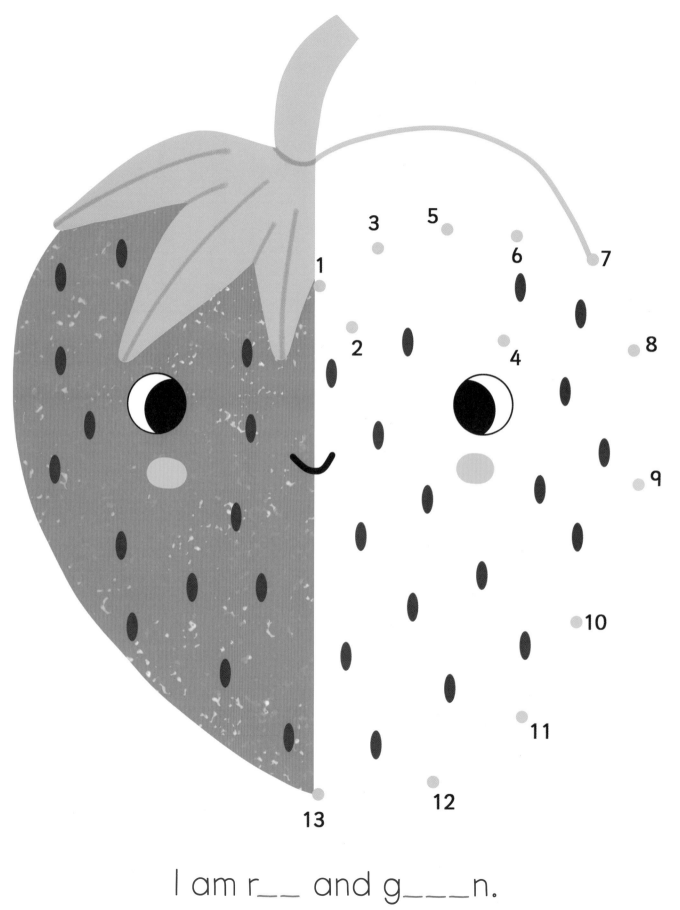

I am r_ _ and g_ _ _ n.

Would you like one of these?

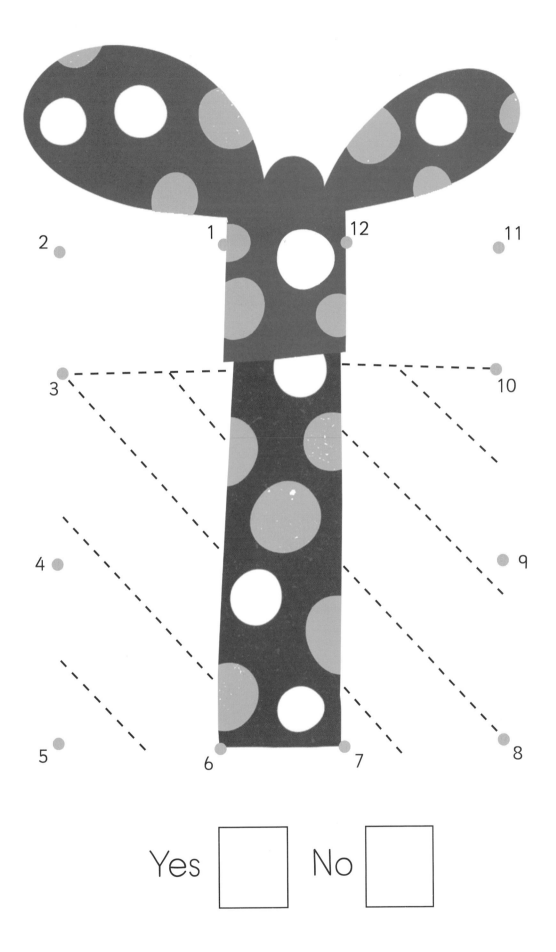

Yes ☐ No ☐

What am I called?

I am called a f__h.

How many spots do I have?

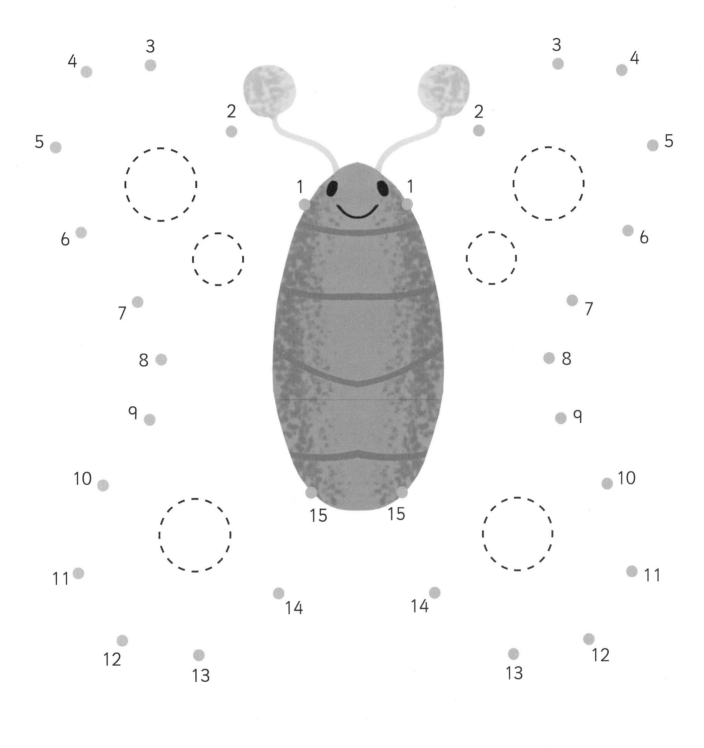

I have ⬜ s___s.

What is this called?

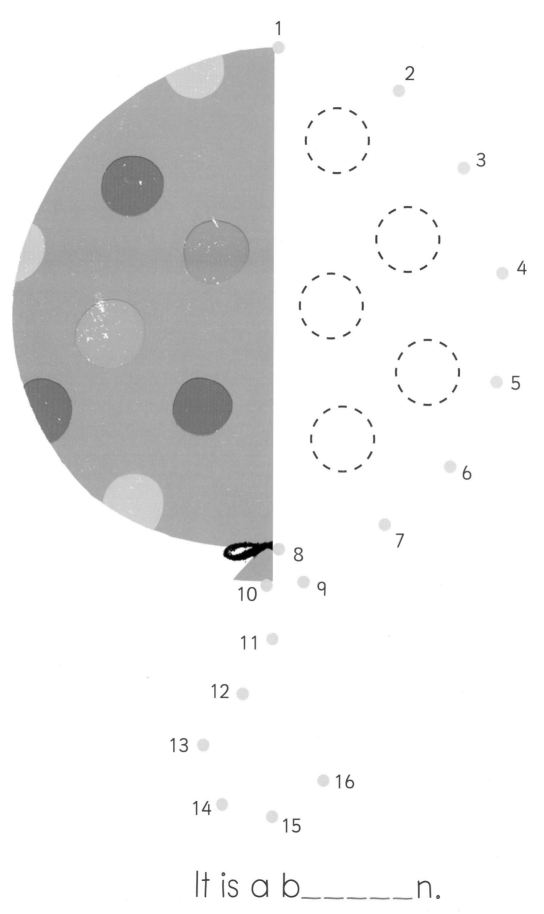

It is a b_____n.

What am I wearing?

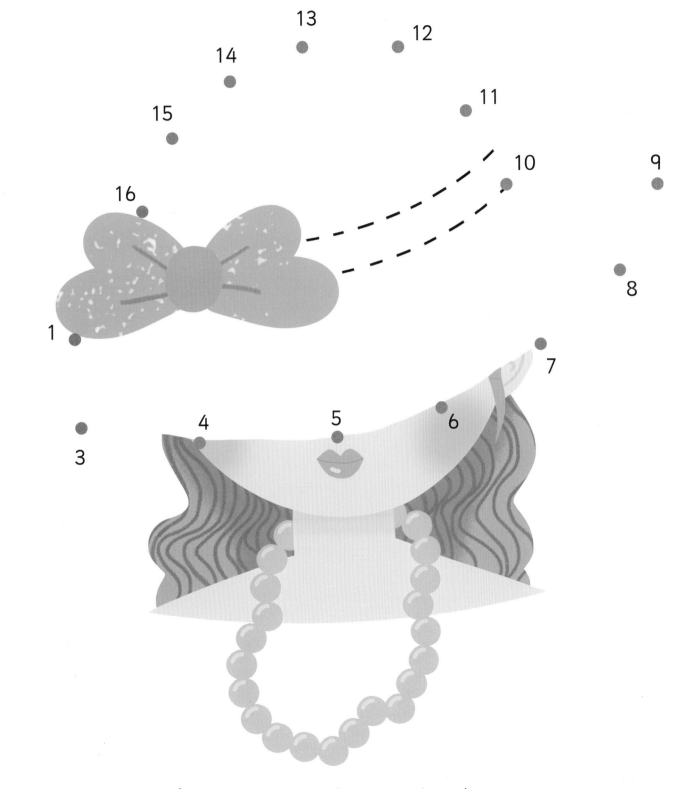

I am wearing a h_t.

Where am I?

4 3 2 1 17 16 15

5 14

6 13

7 12

8 11

9 10

I am in a n__t.

When do you use me?

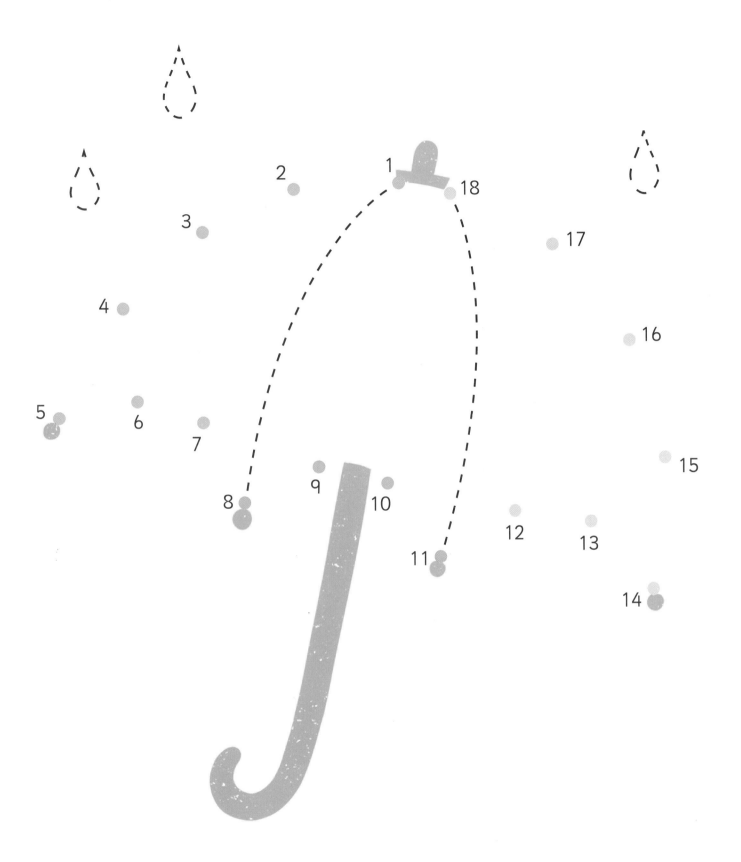

You use me when it is r__n__g.

What am I?

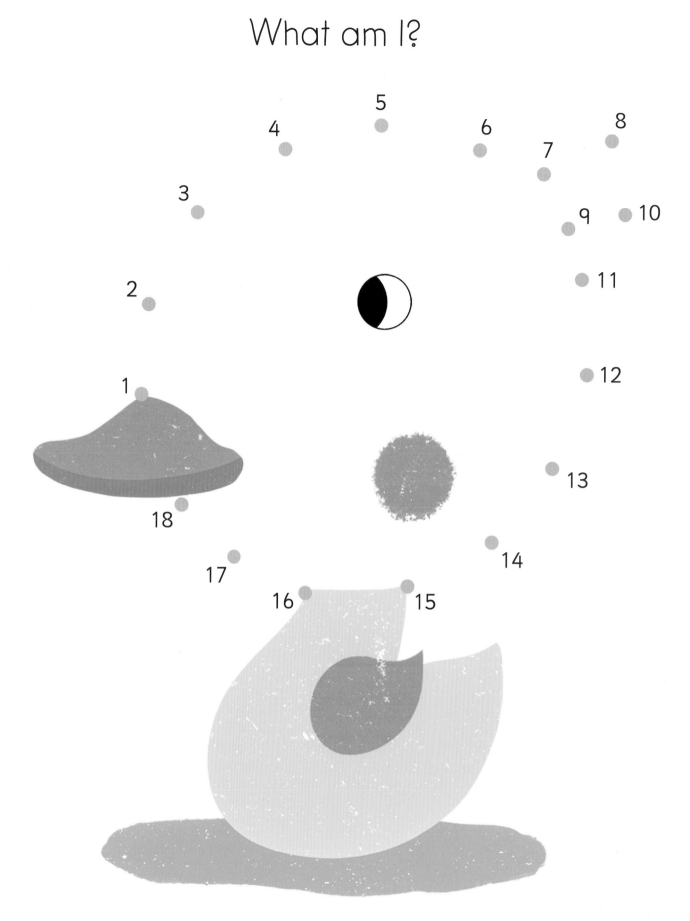

I am a d__k.

How many of these can you see?

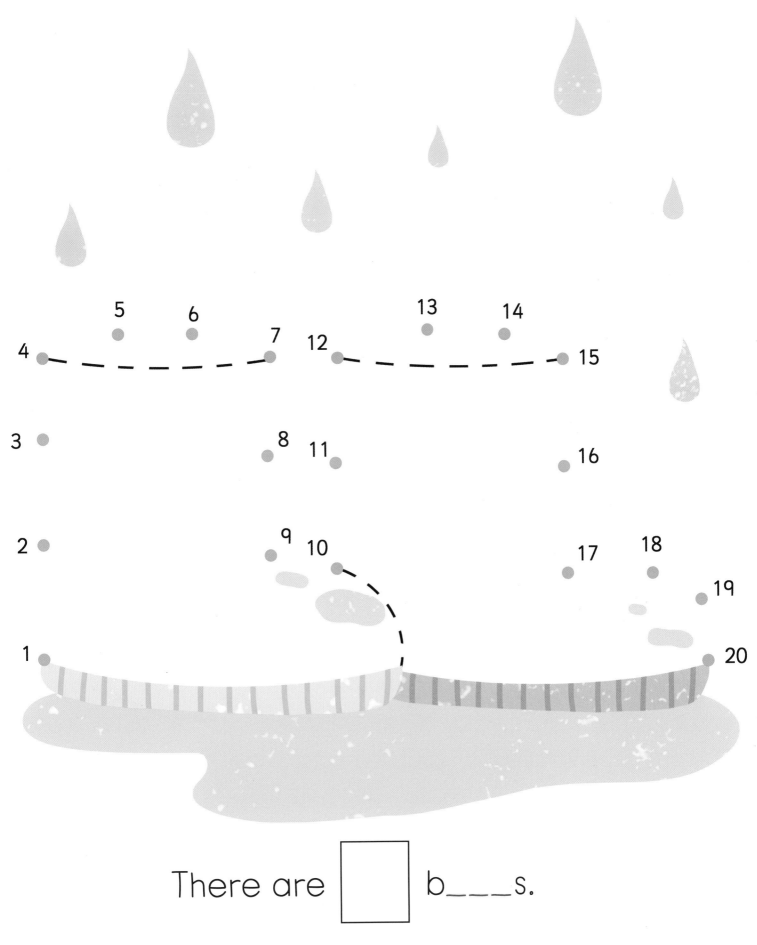

There are ☐ b___s.

What is the spider sitting on?

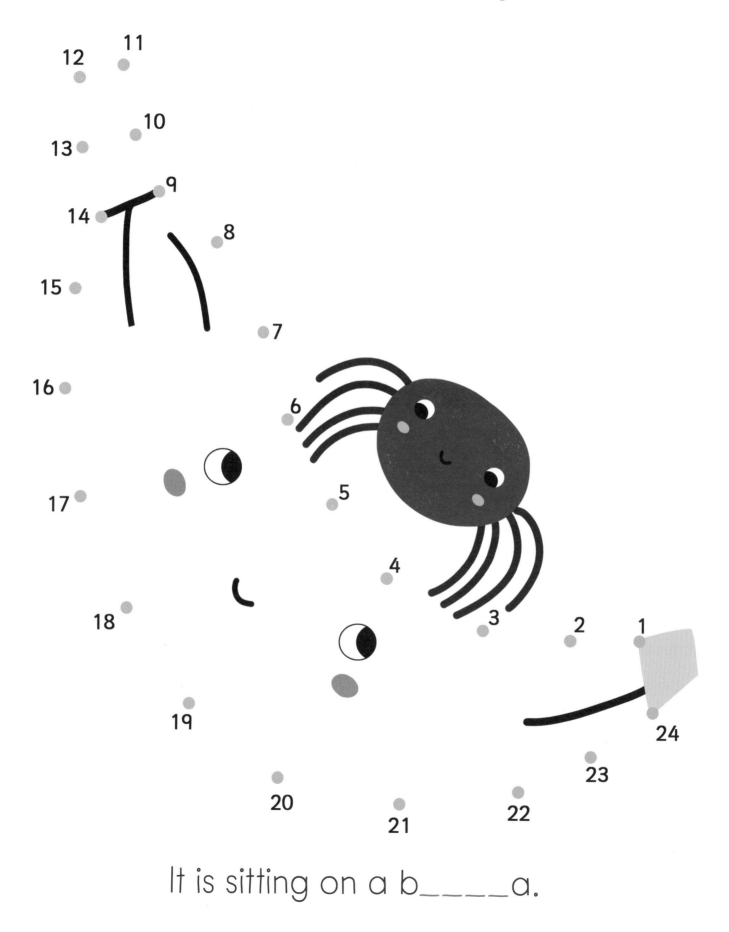

It is sitting on a b_____a.

What am I called?

3
2
1
25
24
23
4
5 6
20
9
21
22
8 7
19
10
12 13
11
14
15
16
18
17

I am a t___y b__r.

How many legs do I have?

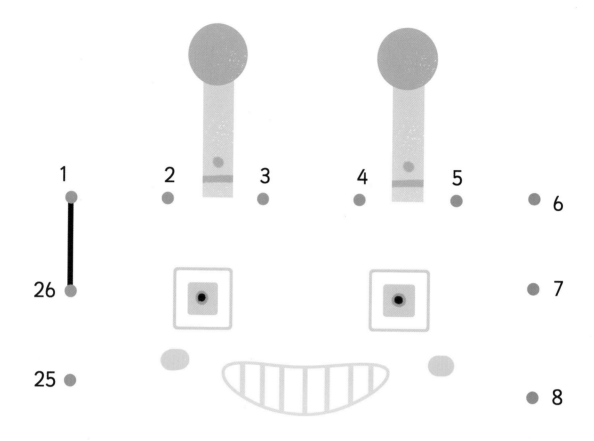

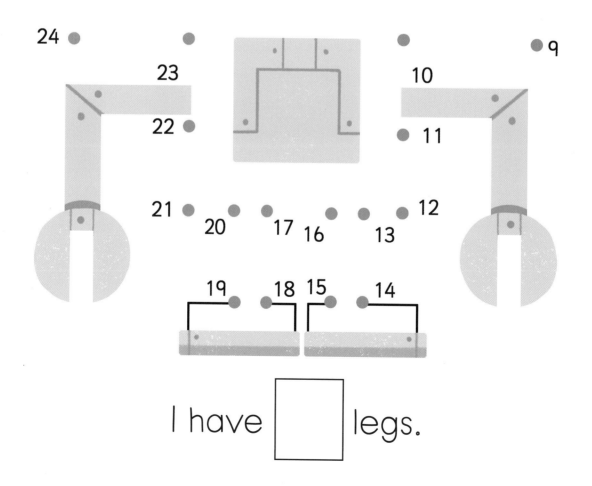

I have ☐ legs.

What's my name?

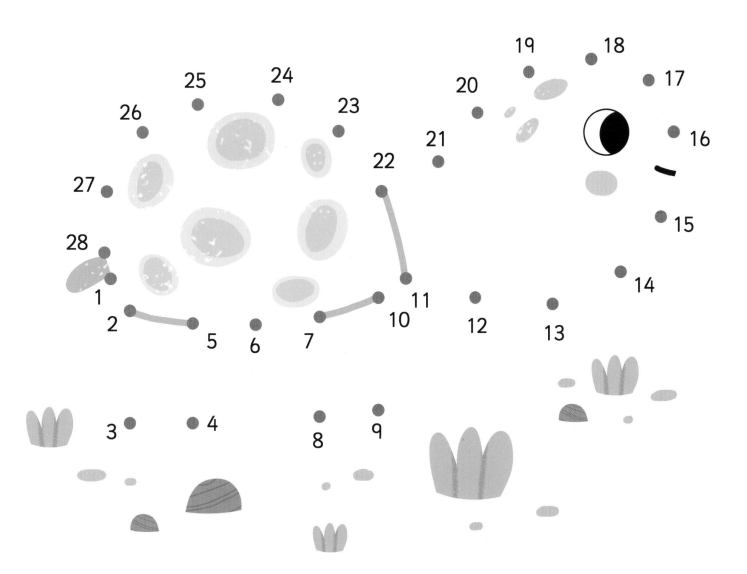

I am a t__t_e.

What am I?

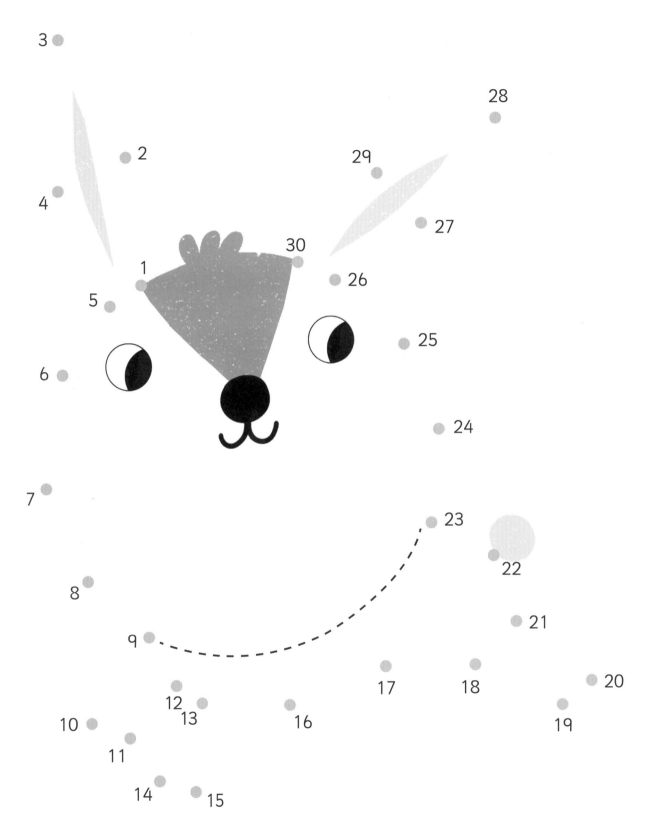

I am a r_ _ _ t.

What is asleep?

I can see a sleeping o_l.

What's this?

It is an a_ _ _n.

What did you find?

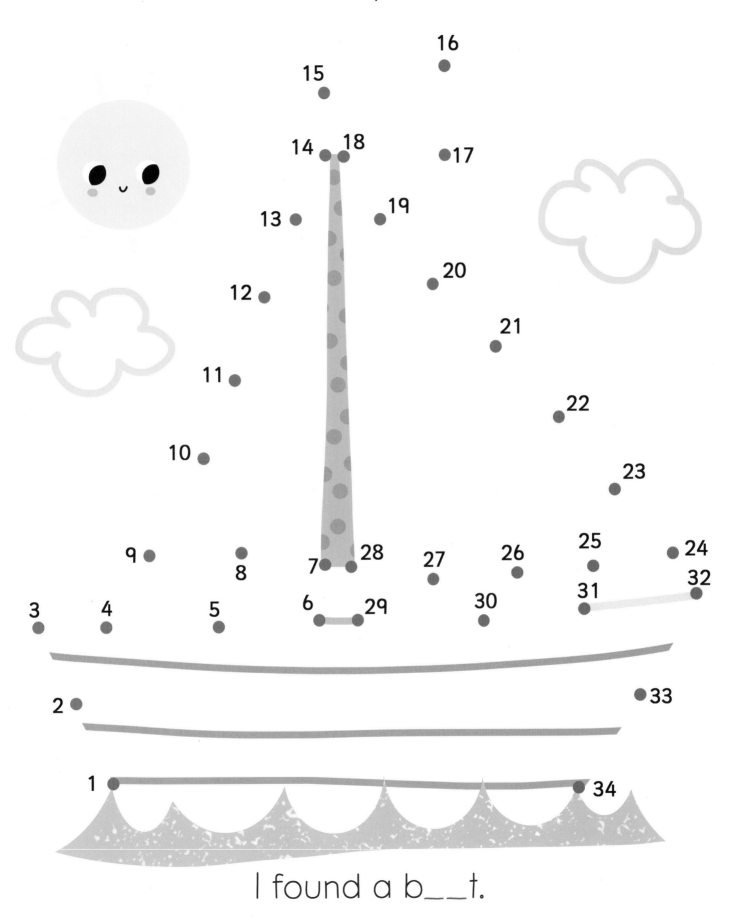

I found a b__t.

What is this called?

It is a u_____n.

How many fish can you see?

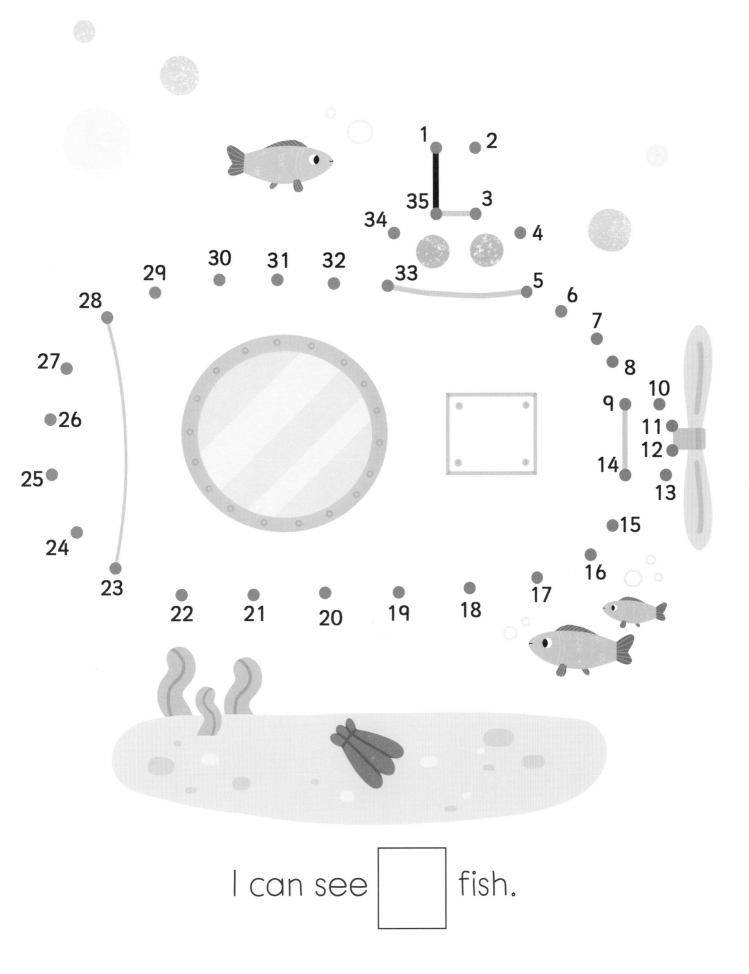

I can see ☐ fish.

What is this?

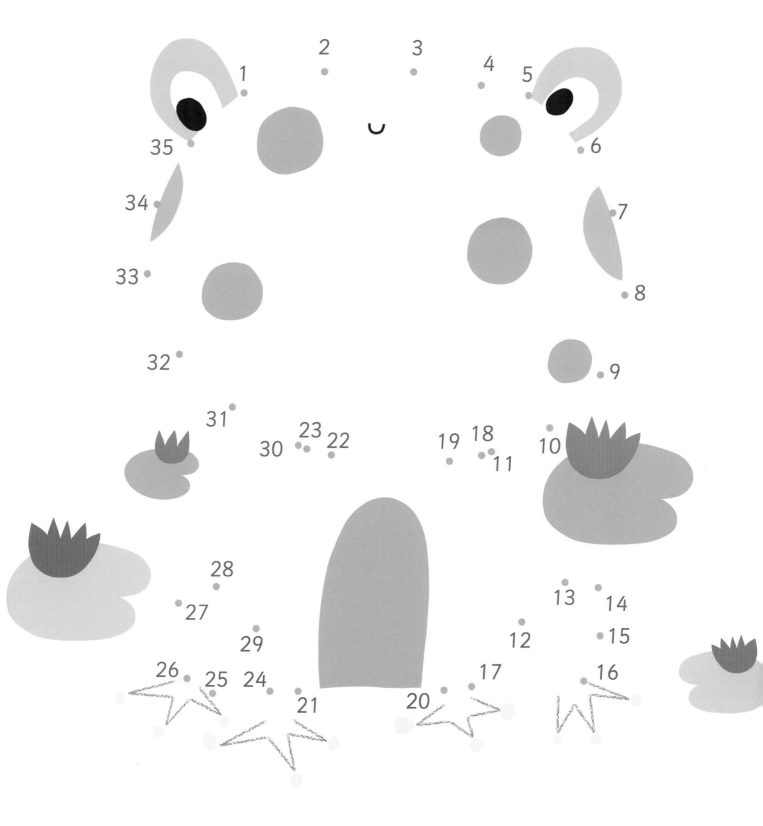

It is a f_ _g.

Where does this go?

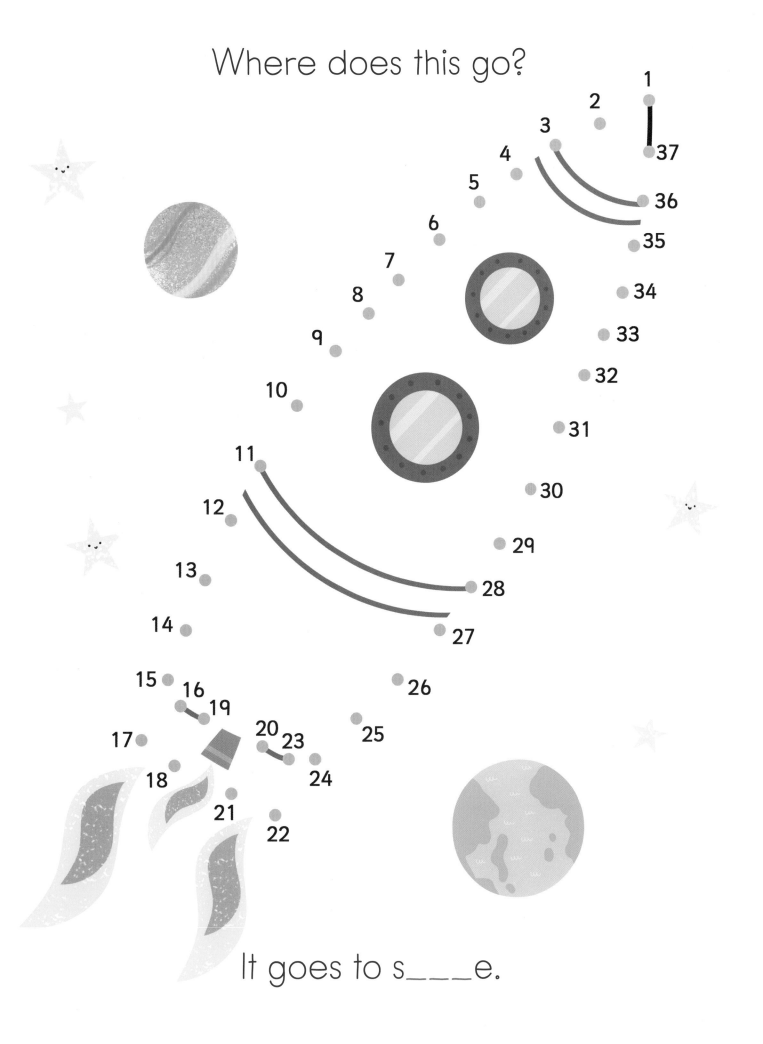

It goes to s___e.

What is this bug eating?

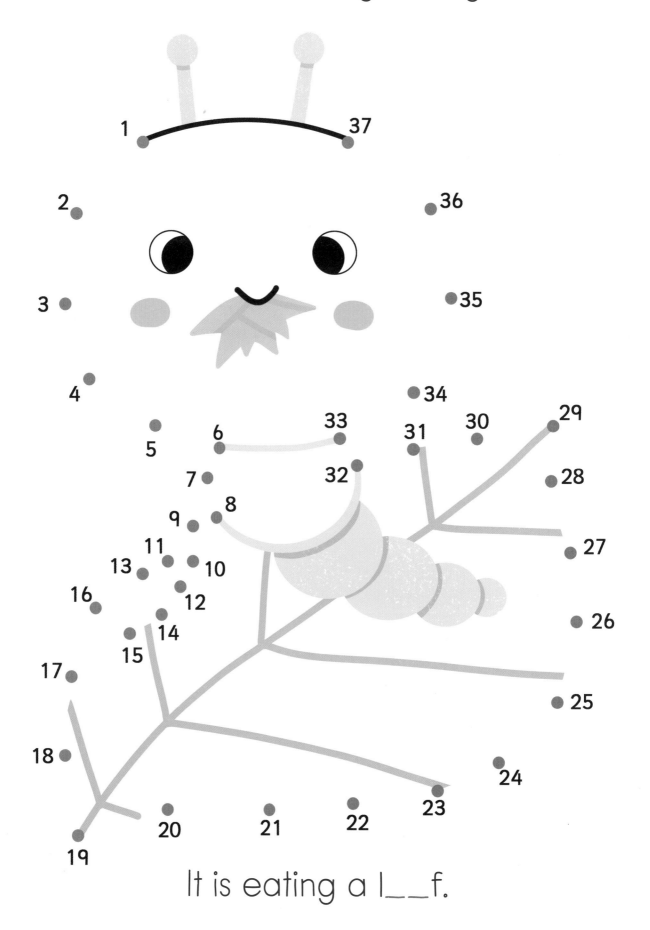

It is eating a l__f.

What am I?

I am a p_g.

How many spots can you see on the ladybug?

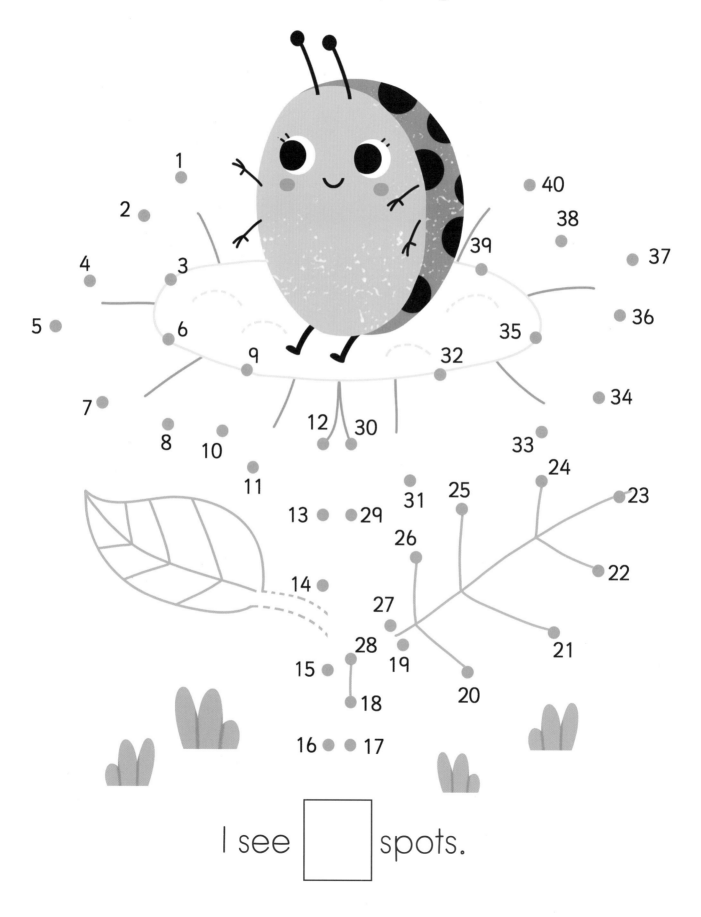

I see ☐ spots.

What is this?

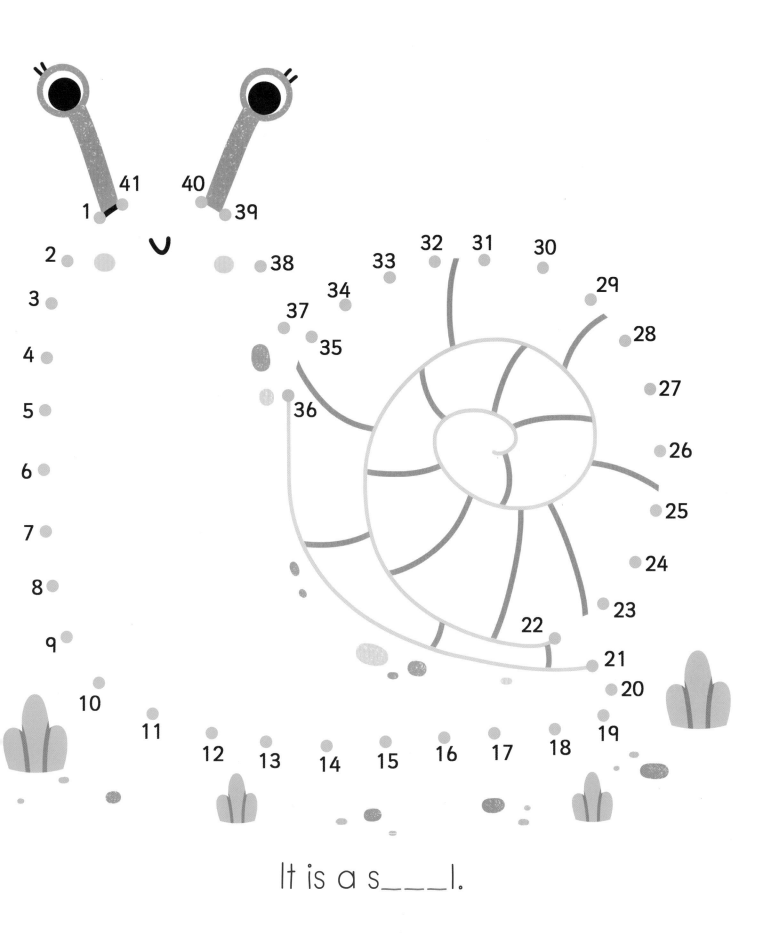

It is a s___l.

Who found a bone?

A d_g found a bone.

What is this?

It is a f_ _m_ _ _o.

What am I wearing on my head?

I am wearing a h_t.

What am I?

I am a c_t.

What am I?

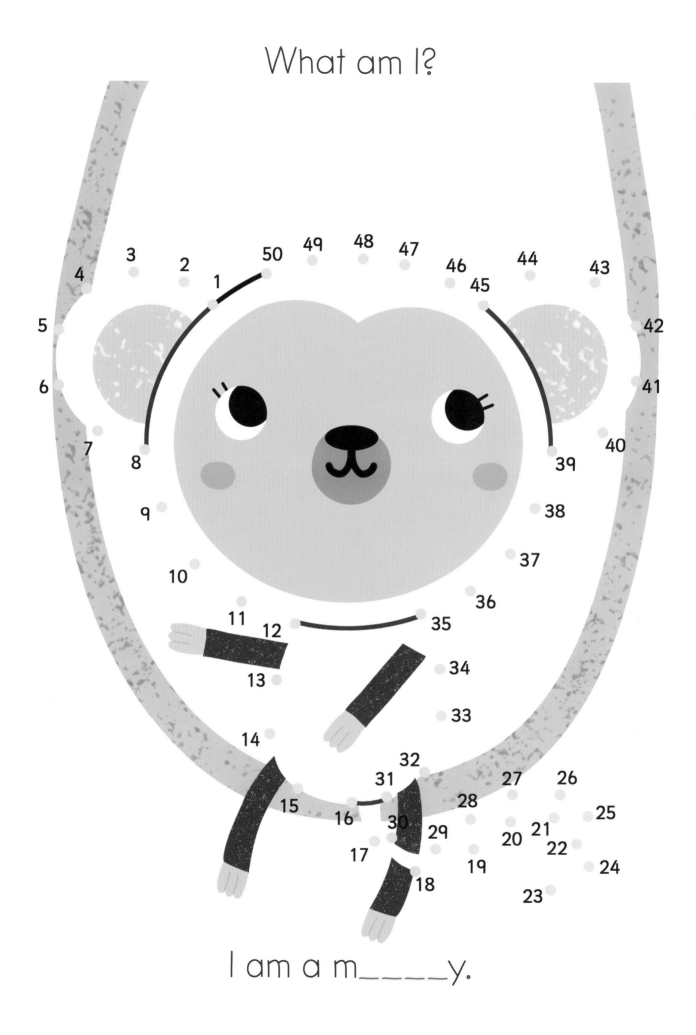

I am a m_ _ _ _y.

What am I?

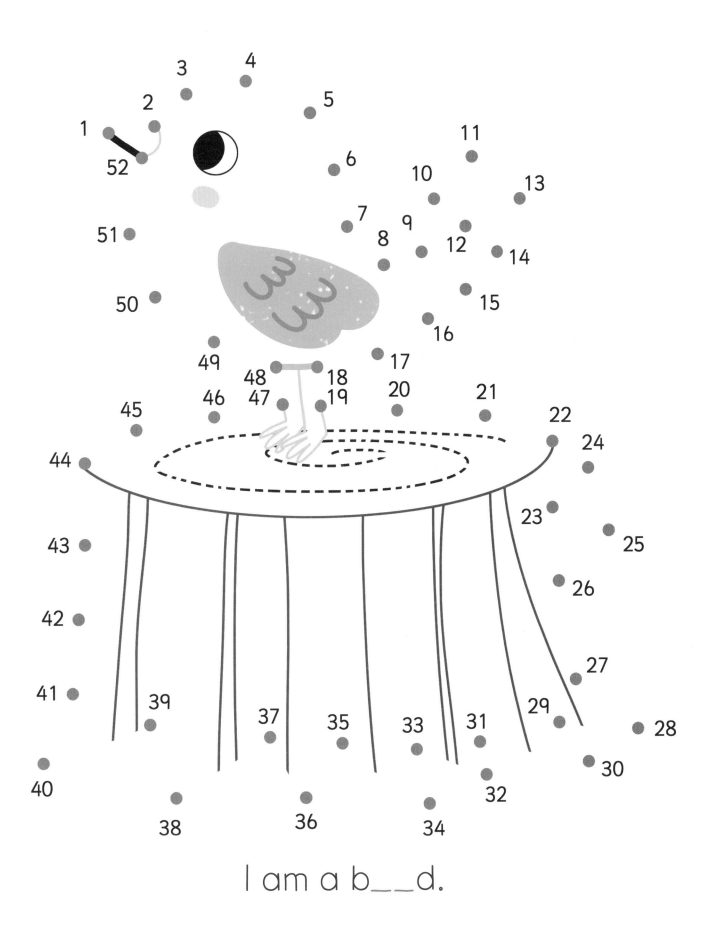

I am a b__d.

Who am I?

I am little r_ _ riding h_ _d.

How many of us can you see?

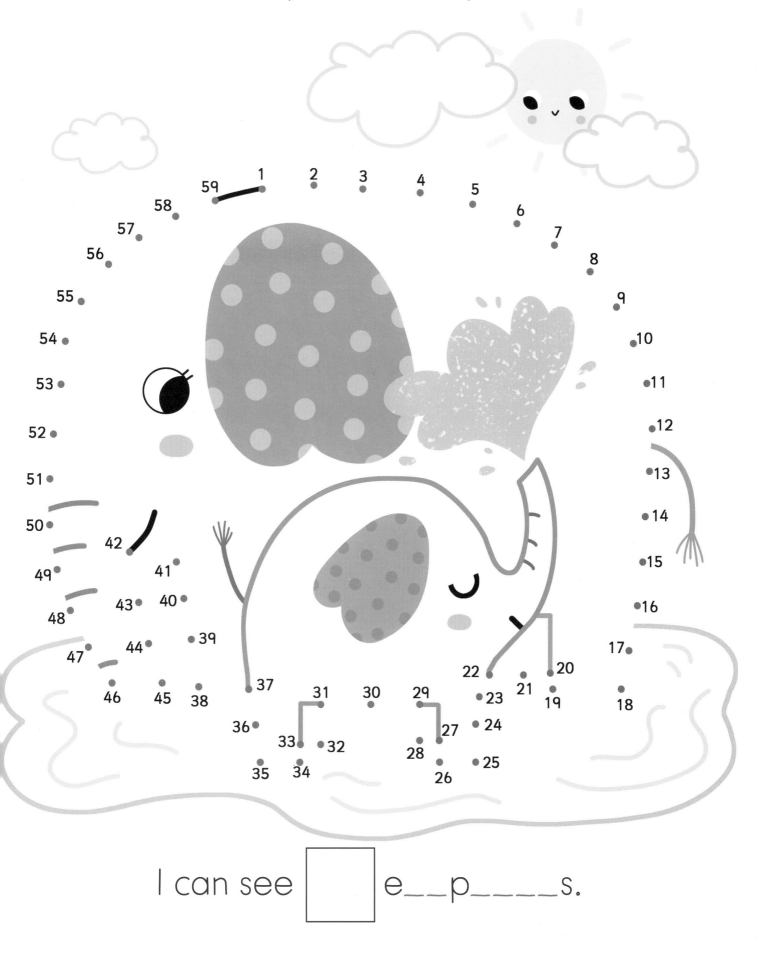

I can see ☐ e__p____s.

What am I?

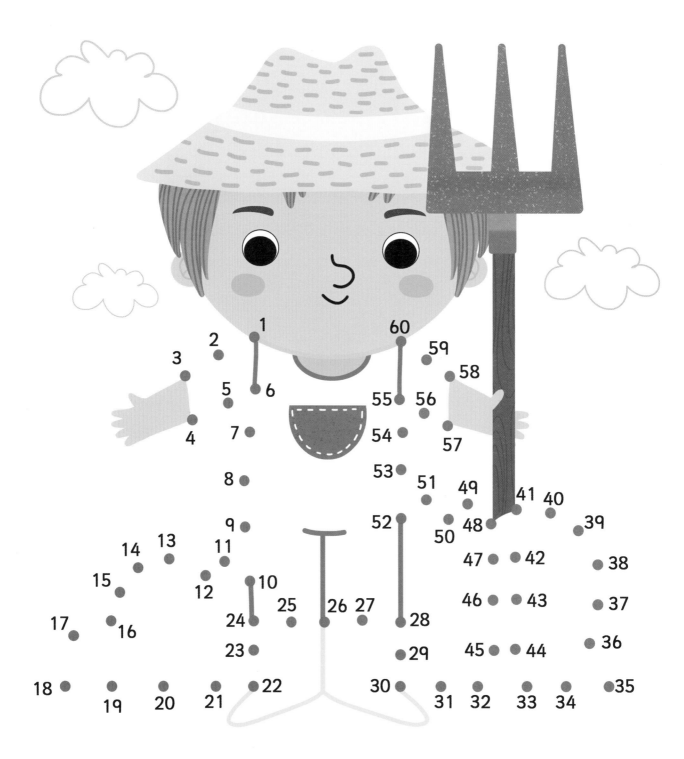

I am a f____r.

Who likes fish?

The b__r likes fish.

How many foals can you see?

I can see ☐ f____.

What is this called?

It is a f__e t___k.

How many tails can you find?

I found ☐ t_ _ _ s.

Who is this?

She is a f____y.

How many animals can you find?

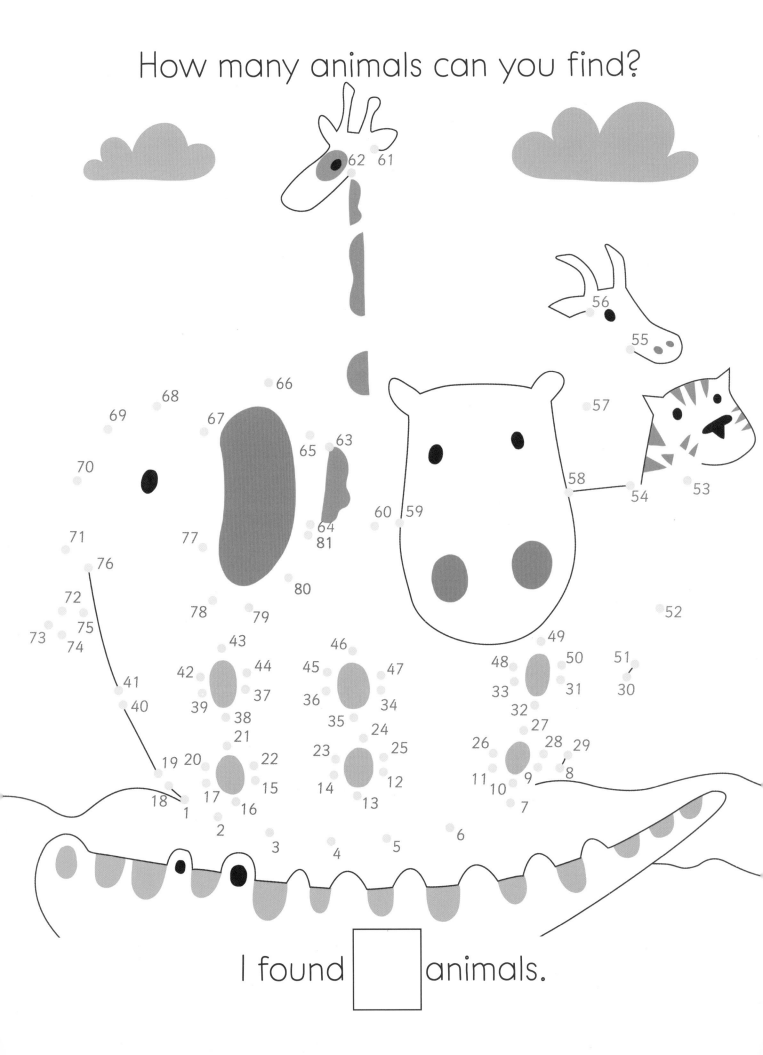

I found ⬚ animals.

Where am I?

I am at the b___h.

How many leaves can you find?

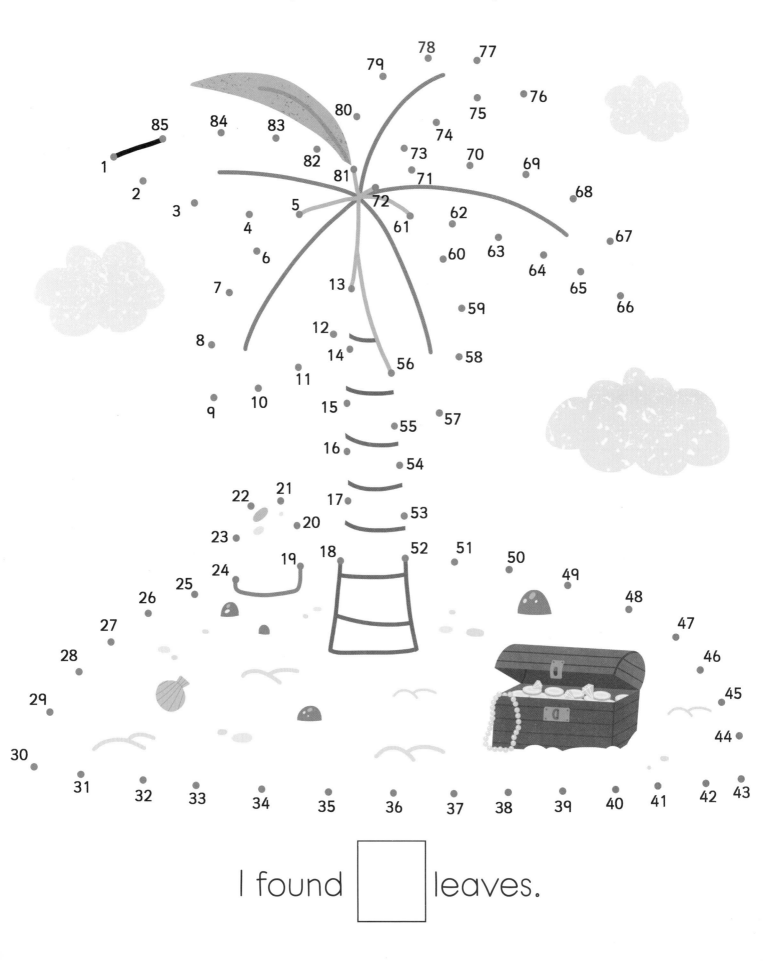

I found ☐ leaves.

Who is asleep?

Baby b__r is asleep.

What did you find?

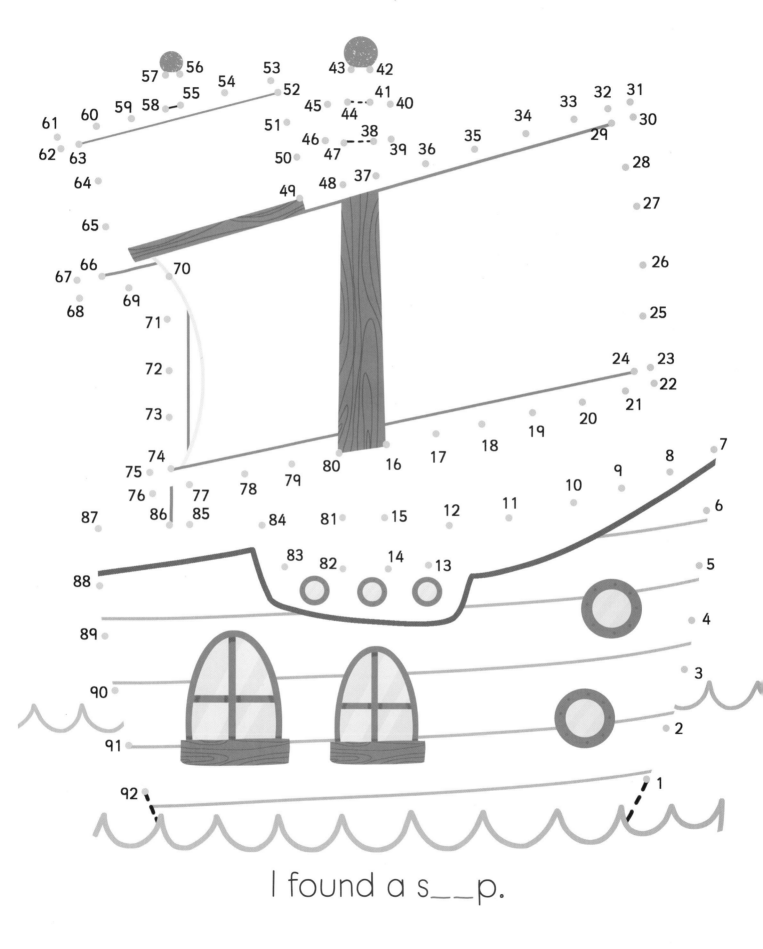

I found a s__p.

How many teeth can you count?

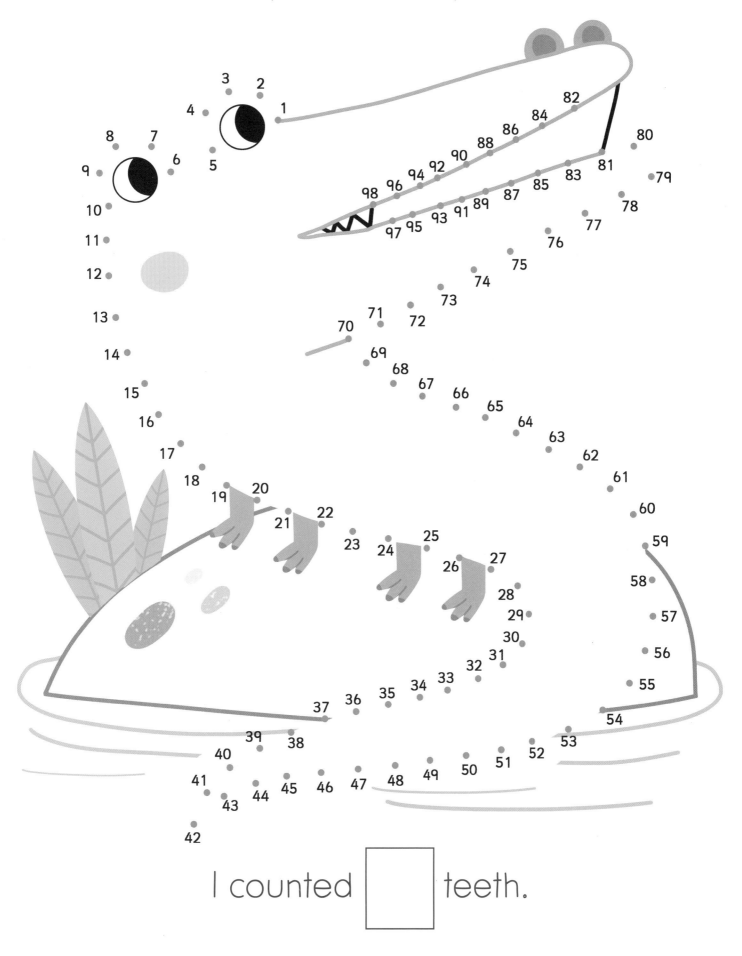

I counted ☐ teeth.

How many houses can you find?

I found ⬚ houses.

What did you find?

I found a d__o____r.

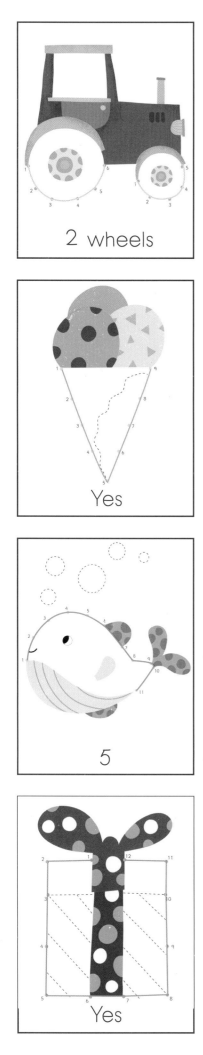

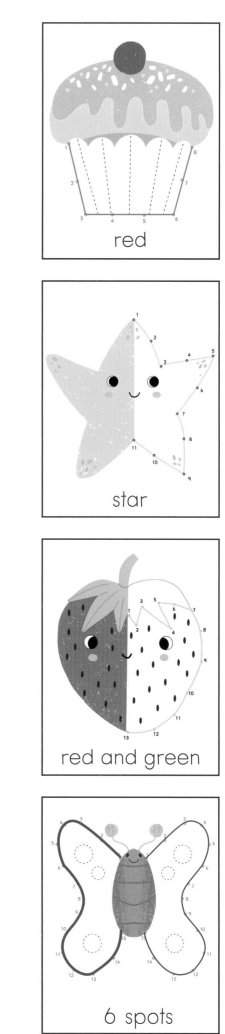

2 wheels

sky

red

Yes

cookies

star

5

heart

red and green

Yes

fish

6 spots

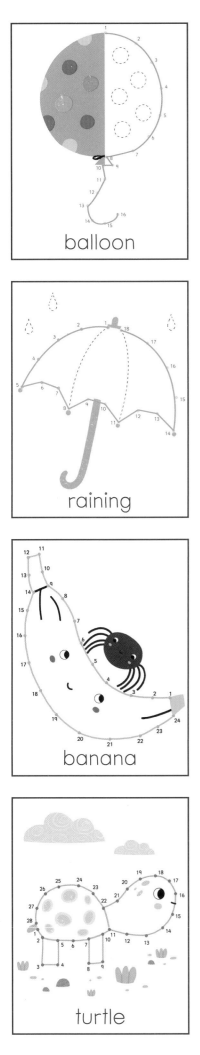

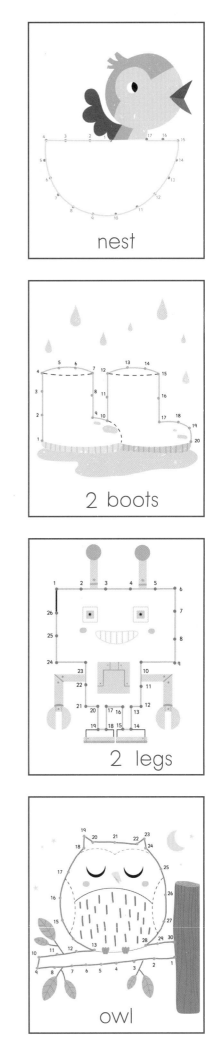

balloon

hat

nest

raining

duck

2 boots

banana

teddy bear

2 legs

turtle

rabbit

owl

alien

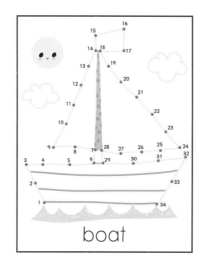

boat

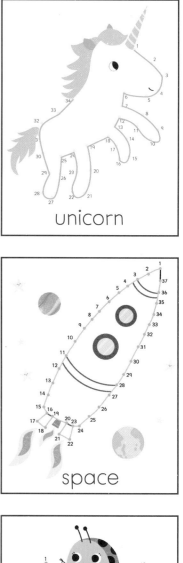

unicorn

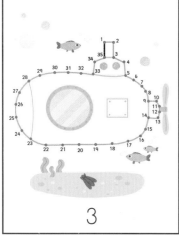

3

frog

space

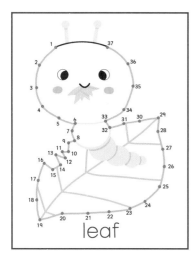

leaf

pig

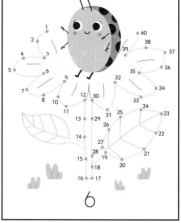

6

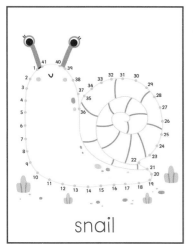

snail

dog

flamingo

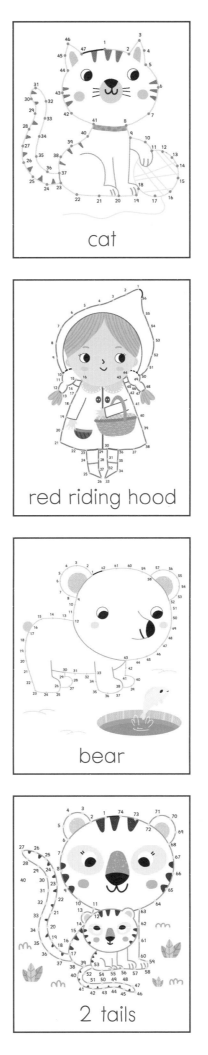

hat

cat

monkey

bird

red riding hood

2 elephants

farmer

bear

1 foal

fire truck

2 tails

fairy

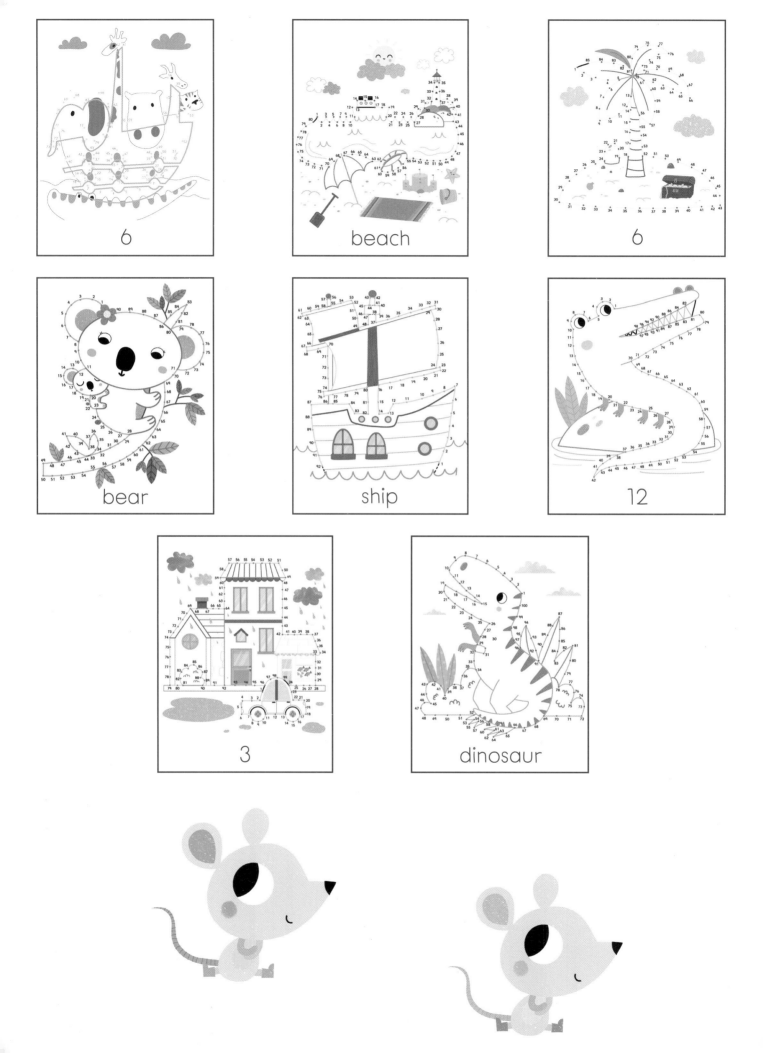

6

beach

6

bear

ship

12

3

dinosaur